anythin

First Facts®

Your Body Systems

Your Skeletal System Works!

by Flora Brett

CAPSTONE PRESS
a capstone imprint

First Facts are published by Capstone Press,
1710 Roe Crest Drive, North Mankato, Minnesota 56003
www.capstonepub.com

Library of Congress Cataloging-in-Publication Data
Brett, Flora, author.
Your skeletal system works! / by Flora Brett.
    pages cm. — (First facts. Your body systems)
Summary: "Engaging text and imformative images help readers learn about their skeletal
system"— Provided by publisher.
Audience: Ages 6–9.
Audience: K to grade 3.
Includes bibliographical references and index.
ISBN 978-1-4914-2068-3 (library binding) — ISBN 978-1-4914-2252-6 (pbk.) —
ISBN 978-1-4914-2274-8 (ebook PDF)
1. Human skeleton—Juvenile literature. 2. Bones—Juvenile literature. 3. Human
physiology—Juvenile literature. I. Title.
QM101.B84 2015
612.7'5—dc23
                                2014023835

Editorial Credits
Emily Raij and Nikki Bruno Clapper, editors; Cynthia Akiyoshi, designer;
Svetlana Zhurkin, media researcher; Laura Manthe, production specialist

Photo Credits
Capstone, 8; Shutterstock: Alila Medical Media, 21, AntiMartina (dotted background),
cover and throughout, Aptyp_koK, cover (top right), back cover, 1 (top right),
BioMedical, 7, Blend Images, 17 (top right), CLS Design, 15, Kjpargeter, 13, oliveromg, 20,
Orange Line Media, 9, Pavel L Photo and Video, 19, Sebastian Kaulitzki, cover, 1, 11,
17 (left), videodoctor, 5

Printed in the United States of America in North Mankato, Minnesota.
092014   008482CGS15

Table of Contents

Strong Skeleton

Your bones are like puzzle pieces. They fit together to make up your skeletal system. But unlike puzzle pieces, your bones are alive! They are living, growing **tissue**.

Bones are light enough to let you move easily. They are also strong enough to hold up your body. Your bones make up your **skeleton**. Your skeleton helps you move, gives you support, and protects your **organs**.

tissue—a layer or bunch of soft material that makes up body parts

skeleton—the bones that support and protect the body of a human or other animal

organ—a part of the body that does a certain job; the heart and lungs are organs

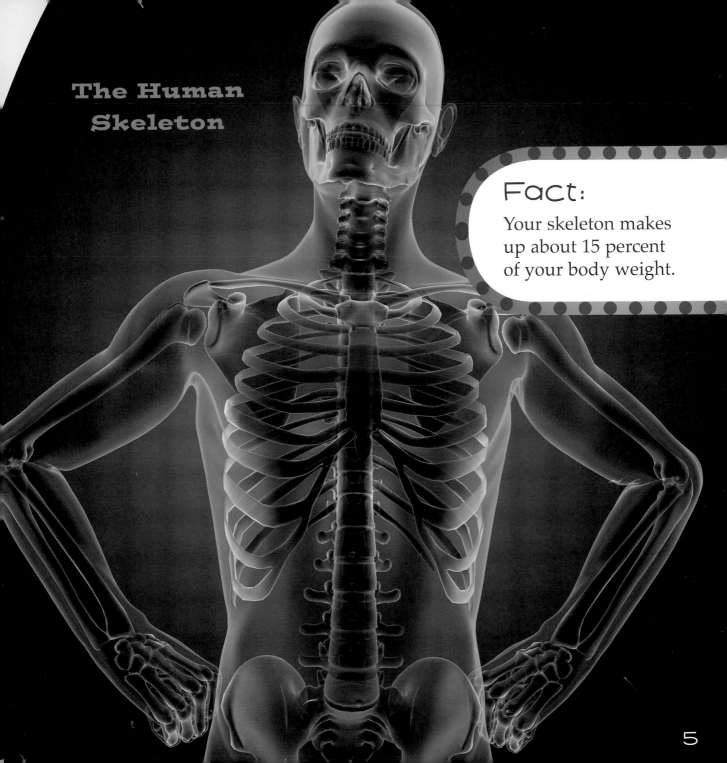

The Human
Skeleton

Fact:
Your skeleton makes
up about 15 percent
of your body weight.

Jobs of the Skeletal System

Your skeleton supports your body and gives it shape. The rib cage protects your heart, lungs, and liver. The skull is like a helmet. It protects your brain.

Important work also happens inside bones. Bone **marrow** makes blood cells. These cells give your body oxygen and fight germs. Bones also store **calcium** and other **minerals**.

marrow—the soft substance inside bones that is used to make blood cells

calcium—a soft, silver-white mineral found in teeth and bones

mineral—a substance found in nature that is not an animal or a plant

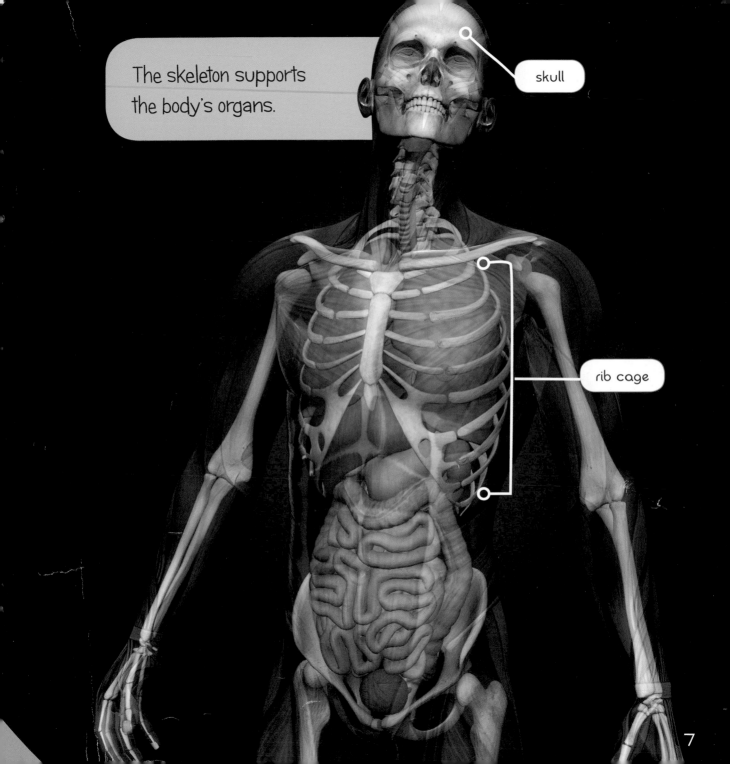

The skeleton supports the body's organs.

skull

rib cage

7

Bone Basics

The outside of bones is made of calcium and other minerals. Calcium makes bones strong. Inside the bone is spongy marrow.

When you were born, you had about 300 bones. As you grow, some bones **fuse** together. They get longer and stronger. By adulthood, you'll have only about 206 bones.

fuse—to join permanently

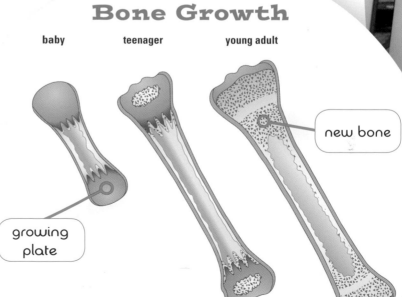

Bone Growth

baby teenager young adult

new bone

growing plate

Fact:

Two hands and wrists have a total of 108 bones. That's more than half the bones in an adult's whole body!

9

Sizes and Shapes of Bones

There are five bone shapes. Long bones form your arms and legs. Short bones in your spine, feet, ankles, hands, and wrists let you bend. Flat bones include the ribs and the skull. They protect your brain and other organs.

Most bones are connected to other bones. But some bones, like your kneecaps, are inside **tendons**. Irregular bones have special shapes and jobs. Your jawbone and your **vertebrae** are irregular bones.

tendon—a strong, thick cord of tissue that joins a muscle to a bone

vertebrae—small bones that make up a backbone

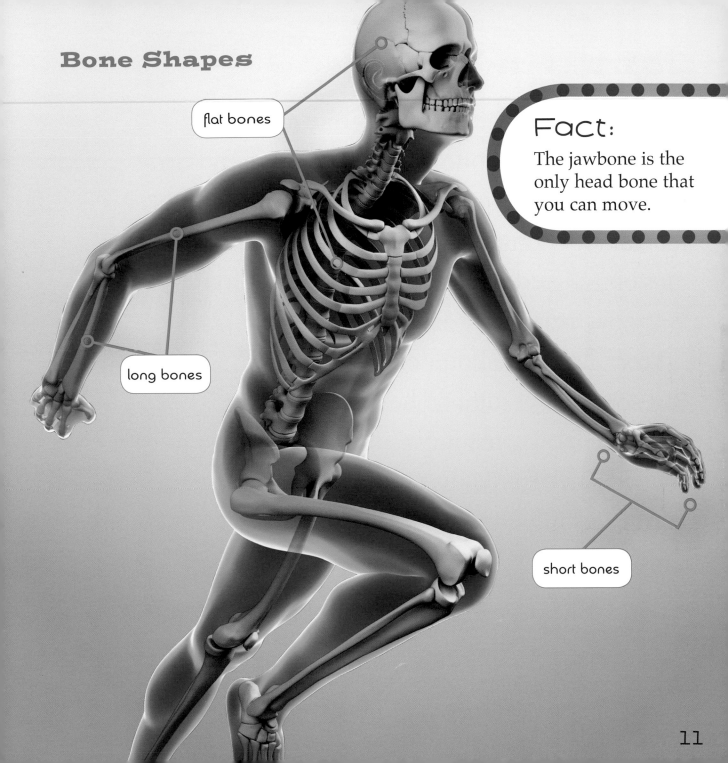

Bone Shapes

flat bones

long bones

short bones

Fact:
The jawbone is the only head bone that you can move.

Joints

Two bones meet at a **joint**. Your body has four joint types. Your elbow is a hinge and pivot joint. It connects the upper and lower arm bones. Hinge joints make your arms move back and forth like a door. Pivot joints help you twist your arms.

Your hips and shoulders are ball-and-socket joints. They let your legs and arms move in circles. Fixed joints don't move. The bones in your skull meet at fixed joints.

Fact:

A person who studies bones and joints is called an orthopedist.

joint—the place where two bones meet; knees, elbows, and hips are joints

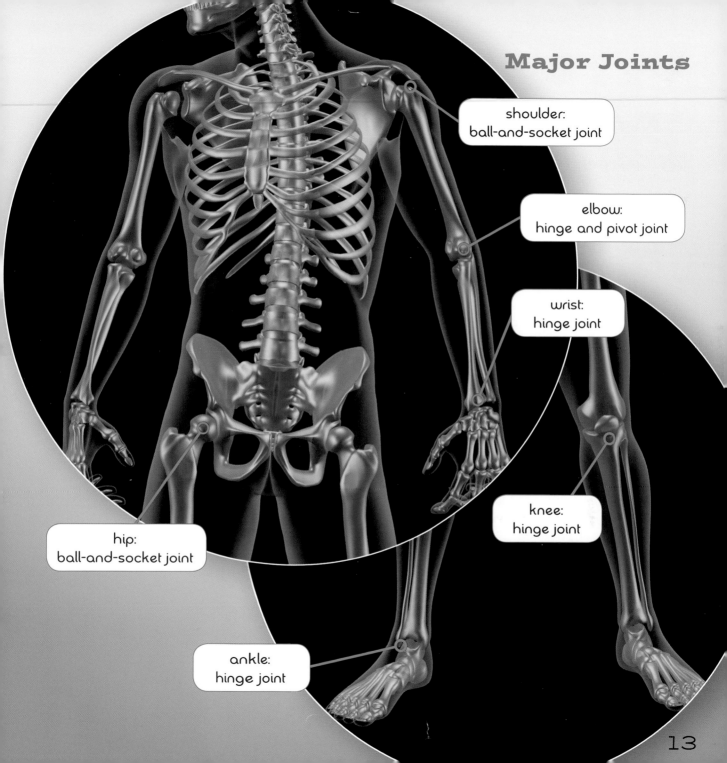

Major Joints

shoulder:
ball-and-socket joint

elbow:
hinge and pivot joint

wrist:
hinge joint

knee:
hinge joint

hip:
ball-and-socket joint

ankle:
hinge joint

13

How Bones Work

Nerves send messages from your brain to your muscles. These messages tell your muscles to move your bones. Muscles pull on the tendons connected to bones. Now your body moves!

Your whole skeleton moves when you play. Long leg bones move you forward. The knee joint bends your leg. Foot bones turn at the ankle joint so you can kick a ball.

nerve—a thin fiber that carries messages between the brain and other parts of the body

Ear bones are the body's smallest bones. They vibrate, or move, to carry sound waves to the brain.

Problems with Bones

Even strong bones can break. Healthy bones break if too much force is put on them. This can happen when you fall.

Broken bones start to heal themselves right away. Blood rushes to the break. Within two weeks, a rubbery **callus** starts to fill in the cracked bone. The callus grows for months. Stronger bone slowly replaces the callus. Finally, the bone is mended.

Fact:
Kids most commonly break the collarbone and the lower arm bones.

callus—a mass of tissue that forms around a broken bone

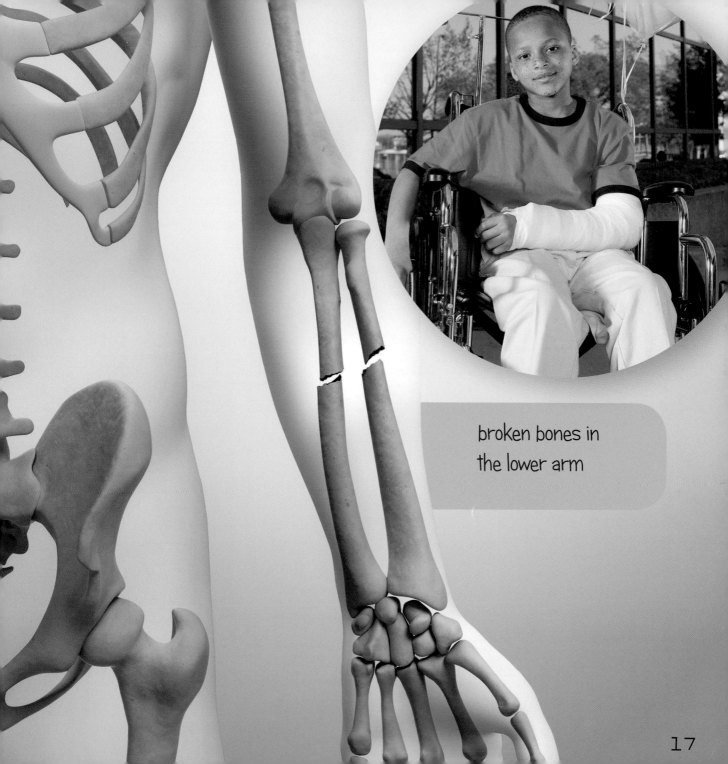

broken bones in
the lower arm

Keeping Bones Healthy

Exercise and good **nutrition** keep bones healthy. Exercise makes bones thicker and stronger. Calcium and vitamin D also strengthen bones. Calcium comes from dairy foods. Vitamin D comes from fish, eggs, and sunlight.

Remember to wear safety gear such as helmets or knee and elbow pads. This gear protects your bones while you exercise.

nutrition—the taking in of food and drinks

Fact:

Kids' bones heal faster and don't break as easily as adults' bones.

Strong Support

Your skeleton is hidden under muscles and skin. But this part of your body is important in everything you do. Your skeletal system helps you stand tall, balance, and make blood. Your bones and muscles work together to support and move your body every day.

Amazing but True!

The humerus is the long bone between your shoulder and your elbow. Have you ever bumped your elbow and had a funny feeling in your arm? This is called "hitting your funny bone." A nerve in your elbow causes the funny feeling. The nerve gets pinched.

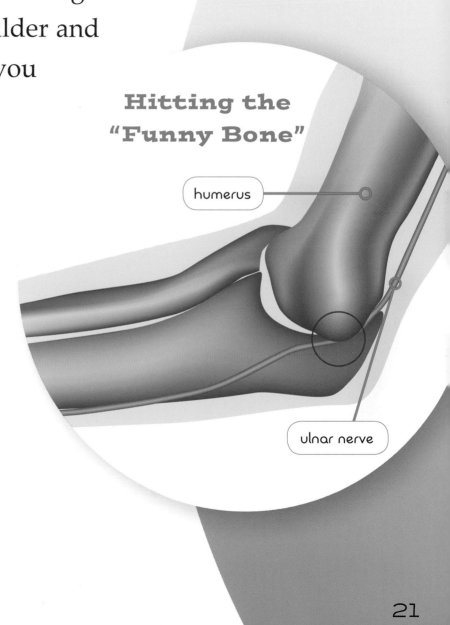

Hitting the "Funny Bone"

humerus

ulnar nerve

Glossary

calcium (KAL-see-uhm)—a soft, silver-white mineral found in teeth and bones

callus (KA-luhs)—a mass of tissue that forms around a broken bone

fuse (FYOOZ)—to join permanently

joint (JOINT)—the place where two bones meet; knees, elbows, and hips are joints

marrow (MA-roh)—the soft substance inside bones that is used to make blood cells

mineral (MIN-ur-uhl)—a substance found in nature that is not an animal or a plant

nerve (NURV)—a thin fiber that carries messages between the brain and other parts of the body

nutrition (noo-TRISH-uhn)—the taking in of food and drinks

organ (OR-guhn)—a part of the body that does a certain job; the heart and lungs are organs

skeleton (SKEL-uh-tuhn)—the bones that support and protect the body of a human or other animal

tendon (TEN-duhn)—a strong, thick cord of tissue that joins a muscle to a bone

tissue (TISH-yoo)—a layer or bunch of soft material that makes up body parts

vertebrae (VUR-tuh-bray)—small bones that make up a backbone

Read More

Clark, Katie. *A Tour of Your Muscular and Skeletal Systems*. First Graphics: Body Systems. North Mankato, Minn.: Capstone Press, 2013.

Tieck, Sarah. *Skeletal System*. Buddy Books: Body Systems. Edina, Minn.: ABDO Pub., 2011.

Wood, Lily. *Skeletons*. Scholastic Readers. New York: Scholastic, 2011.

Internet Sites

FactHound offers a safe, fun way to find Internet sites related to this book. All of the sites on FactHound have been researched by our staff.

Here's all you do:
Visit *www.facthound.com*
Type in this code: 9781491420683

Super-cool stuff! Check out projects, games and lots more at **www.capstonekids.com**

Critical Thinking
Using the Common Core

1. Different types of joints allow for different movements. What are the four joint types? What does each type do? (Key Ideas and Details)

2. Can you remember a time when you or a friend broke a bone? How can you keep your bones healthy and strong? (Integration of Knowledge and Ideas)

3. How do bones heal themselves after a break? (Key Ideas and Details)

Index